RELEASING ANGER

GW00669807

BY LIZ ADAMSON

THE ULTIMATE GUIDES TO EMOTIONAL FREEDOM

RELEASING ANGER

by Liz Adamson

Published by Diviniti Publishing Ltd

P.O. BOX 313, West Malling,

Kent,   ME19 5WE

Tel: 01732 220373

Email admin@hypnosisaudio.com

Website: www.hypnosisaudio.com

ISBN 1 901923 43 6

2nd Edition

Cover Image by Diane Frost

ANGER

Anger is probably the most destructive force there is on Earth. It is a by-product of fear and it is at the root of war, divorce, aggression, drug addiction, vandalism, abuse and most of the self destructive behaviour that we have.

Most people are very uncomfortable with their own and other people's anger and this is why the problem is rarely addressed and dealt with. We may allude to it and lament its existence but few people are willing to go in and do what is needed to safely release it.

If children are taught to understand and release their anger without hurting anyone, we could avert many of the problems that occur in the adult world.

However it is never too late to release the anger that we have stored away and be free to enjoy life to the maximum. I will endeavour to explain the anatomy of anger and give practical ways of releasing it.

WHAT IS ANGER?

Anger is a response to a situation where someone either: **DOES SOMETHING WE DON'T WANT THEM TO DO** or **DOESN'T DO SOMETHING WE WANT THEM TO DO.**

If we look at the times that we have felt angry, the situation will usually fit into one or other of these categories.

Anger is almost always aimed at a person or God, whereas fear is usually aimed at a situation. This is what makes anger more difficult to cope with. It is personal, it feels like it is an attack.

When we feel angry as adults, it is rarely about the person who has triggered it. It is about the first time we experienced that situation in childhood. For instance, a bartender who gets a fist in the face for refusing a customer another drink is actually paying the price for a parent who refused that person more ice cream or another sweet in childhood. The situation will mirror the original cause and bring to the surface the feelings and reactions that were created at the time.

ANGER AND THE CHILD

To understand the anatomy of anger and how it manifests in our lives, we need to go back to the development of the child.

Babies naturally know how to deal with emotions. Whatever they feel they express instantly. If a baby is upset, it cries. If it is angry, it yells and screams and if it is happy it smiles and laughs. The baby will express its feelings until they have the desired effect of communicating its need to the carer. At this point the feelings have gone and there is no residue left and the baby is free to feel its next emotion. A baby also learns that if it expresses anger due to the parent not doing what it wants or doing what it doesn't want, then the parent will usually change its behaviour to fit in with the baby's desires.

This state of affairs may last up until the baby is about eighteen months old when the demands increase and the parent begins to put its foot down.

Suddenly at the age of two, the child finds that not only is the parent not giving into its demands but is making it quite clear that anger is not an acceptable emotion to express. Indeed, most toddlers learn that anger is met with punishment and the anger of the parent. From this point on, we learn to suppress our anger. This does not mean that we don't feel the anger but we are not afforded the opportunity to release it. Every time a situation arises that incites our anger, we have to suppress it and store it in the body.

Anger is a **CHILD** response. When we feel anger as an adult, it is still a childish emotion. We want to yell and scream, hit out, stamp our foot and shout **I HATE YOU**, exactly as a two year old would do. When the child in us is angry, the adult in us often responds just as our parents might have done. We are told that we are bad, wrong, even wicked for having this feeling and the thoughts that come with it. When a child is angry and hits its mother, it does not hurt much. When the child in a fully grown man is angry and hits out, someone could be killed or badly injured.

It is essential to teach children and the child within us that anger is not wrong but the **INAPPROPRIATE** expression of anger is not a good idea. When a child is angry because it is not allowed another biscuit or it has to go to bed, it is important that the parent validates the child's right to be angry and shows it how to express it safely without actually giving in to the child's demands and manipulation.

As we grow older the amount of anger that we have to store in the body grows and builds up. When we suppress our negative emotions, we are also forced to suppress our positive ones. Love, laughter, joy, peace and play are often forfeited when we do not express our anger and pain.

POSITIONS OF ANGER

There are three positions where anger will be in the body. It will be suppressed, on the surface or expressed.

When anger is suppressed, the last thing we are actually feeling is anger. This is the most common position for us to find anger. When we first experience the anger it is very uncomfortable and we look for ways to push it down so that we no longer need to feel it. Many people who suppress their anger will often believe that they have **NO** anger. In reality they may have far more than other people and are astounded if and when it eventually emerges. When anger is suppressed we may not feel it but it can do untold damage to the physical body.

When anger is on the surface we are aware of it and may feel it a great deal of the time. It is easy for others to see that we are angry, it is almost tangible.

RELEASING ANGER

We are often very volatile with short fuses. We may use our anger to control other people. It is important to note that feeling our anger and releasing it are two very different things. We do not get rid of our anger just by feeling it. However, we cannot release it until we are in touch with it. When it is suppressed, it cannot be removed unless it first comes to the surface. When anger is on the surface we often go over the same ground in our mind. We relive the whole situation and fuel our anger by hanging onto it.

The **SAFE** expression of anger is what we are aiming for. Once anger is on the surface, the next step is to express it and let it go. As soon as anger is released we no longer feel it, it is gone. When the anger is removed we often do not remember the original cause of the anger. Releasing this toxic feeling **WILL SET US FREE**.

ANGER
AND DEPRESSION

Depression is something that effects almost all of us at some point in our lives, to a greater or lesser extent. Even the most positive among us may have feelings of depression after a big life changing event like death, birth, redundancy or divorce. There are some people that are dogged by depression and it effectively rules their lives.

DEPRESSION IS USUALLY ANGER AND PAIN TURNED INWARDLY AGAINST THE SELF.

When the anger begins to emerge from the suppressed position to come to the surface, we try to prevent it from reaching our consciousness by **DEPRESSING** it back down. Usually the amount of anger that is emerging is too overwhelming to be able to do this and so we are stuck in this emotional no mans land. There will usually be a trigger for the emergence of the anger.

RELEASING ANGER

When we are depressed we do not **FEEL** angry. We may feel nothing. We are tired and apathetic. This is because the amount of energy it takes to keep such a powerful force under wraps is enormous. There is no energy left for us. We are unable to laugh, feel joy, or have fun. When we suppress one emotion to this extent we will end up suppressing all emotion.

With depression we cannot be bothered with anything or anybody. When there is so much anger within us it will overshadow any love we have for ourselves and others. Most of our behaviour while depressed will be self-destructive.

There are forms of depression that are created on a physical chemical level and these cases may need to be treated with pills or some other kind of medical intervention. However, most cases can be almost instantly alleviated by the safe expression of the anger that is trying to surface. When we take pills to deal with depression iwe are pushing the feelings down to a suppressed position where they affect the body and will emerge again at a later date.

ANGER AND AGGRESSION

Aggression occurs when we project our anger onto others. This is clearly the opposite dynamic to depression. Aggression is extremely destructive. In some cases we physically hurt people or destroy property. More commonly we hurt people emotionally with our words and demeanour.

It is important to note that aggressive people do not release their anger by expressing it in this way. If anything it merely serves to fuel the underlying cause of the anger. With aggression it will be dumped on anyone that gets in the way. Road rage is a typical example of this.

With aggression there may be a tendency to see everyone else to be at fault for whatever happens to us. We rarely take responsibility for the part we play in creating everything that occurs in our lives. Revenge may even play a part in this. We want to punish the person we perceive to have stood in our way or done something to us. If we cannot do this we may punish someone else instead.

Aggressive people will often have had a difficult childhood and they hold on to every incident or slight that occurred. There could also be a pattern of getting attention from their negative behaviour.

Anger comes from a position of powerlessness. However when we are aggressive, it may give an illusion of power. People are frightened of us and the sheer energy of the aggression makes us feel strong. This therefore perpetuates the negative behaviour. We are often very loathe to change our aggressive patterns for fear of being weak and powerless.

ANGER AND ILLNESS

Anger is a very toxic emotion and if it is suppressed in the body for any length of time, can do untold damage to the physical body. It may be at the root of many illnesses and degenerative conditions. Dis-ease in the body on an emotional level is going to create disease in the body on a physical level.

Anger plays a large part in many ailments like cancer, arthritis, cystitis, skin problems, inflammations and many other problems. When we release anger, it can play a huge role in healing the body, so much so that it should be included in any treatment, particularly with those conditions that are life threatening. It is not uncommon to see some pain and illnesses disappear overnight after doing anger work.

HOW TO RECOGNISE ANGER

When we have a great deal of anger suppressed in the body, we will not be **FEELING** the anger but it may be manifesting in our lives in many different ways. When these symptoms show themselves it is usually because the anger is wanting to surface and we may unconsciously employ various means to try and prevent the awareness of the feelings. Many of these symptoms get in the way of our being able to live life to the full, so it very important to acknowledge that they are getting in our way and to take the necessary steps to release the anger and put our lives back on track.

Here are some of the ways in which anger shows itself unconsciously.

1) Extreme tiredness and apathy. Not wanting to get up and face the day.

RELEASING ANGER

2) Can't be bothered to do anything productive or creative.

3) Finding the every day jobs of life to be a struggle.

4) Wanting to escape from ourselves and dealing with our lives by being engrossed in television, videos, computers or books.

5) Craving unhealthy foods like chocolate, sweet things, junk food or red meat.

6) Using alcohol, cigarettes or drugs to deaden and suppress feelings.

7) Can't be bothered to make an effort with our appearance. (In extreme cases not washing or bathing.)

8) Wanting to be on our own. Not feeling like socialising or talking to people.

9) Not doing anything that would be good for us like exercising or getting help from a therapist.

10) Slamming doors, this may be more noticeable with car doors.

RELEASING ANGER

11) Finding that we wake up with our jaw firmly clenched.
12) Coughing. When we find that we have a dry cough without having a cold.
13) Finding that we cut or burn ourselves, particularly the hands.
14) Clumsiness. When we often break things, have accidents and bump into things.
15) Untidiness. When we allow our environment to become cluttered, untidy and dirty.
16) Procrastination. Not keeping up with paying bills or paperwork.
17) Not feeling like having sex.
18) Not wanting to make eye contact with the people that we are experiencing the anger for.
19) Not wanting to talk about our feelings in case it triggers off our anger.
20) Avoiding any conflict or rows.

If we are displaying more that three of four of these symptoms, there is probably some anger that is ready to emerge and be expressed.

DENIAL OF ANGER

Few people have any concept of the amount of anger that we hold in our bodies. However there are some among us who adamantly refuse to admit that they have any anger at all. I have never come across anyone who has **NO** anger.

Medical studies have shown that those in denial of their anger are in far more danger of contracting illnesses and life threatening conditions, than those who are in touch with their anger.

In social situations those in denial of anger will often assume a facade of niceness to disguise their inner anger. However, sensitive people will pick up on the anger and will wonder at the mixed signals coming from that individual. These mixed messages will prevent us from getting close to that person because every time we tune into them, we will feel their anger and be uncomfortable. There is also a tendency for us to mirror each other, so someone who is in denial of their anger may find that they attract many angry people into their environment.

When we choose to lead a spiritual or "good" life, anger becomes a dirty word. We are told that love is what we must aspire to. Yet it is very difficult to love when there is so much anger inside us. It is only when we acknowledge the anger and let it go that we are able to work on love. We cannot love others until we learn to love ourselves and we will find it very difficult to love ourselves if we are angry. It is like a ramshackle house that is filled with junk and allowed to decay inside and yet the only work we do on it is to renovate the exterior.

When we are in denial of our anger, we can be a danger to ourselves as well as others. We may reach a point where we can no longer control our emotions and we could explode at inopportune moments.

PARENTS AND ANGER

Our anger is created in childhood. Anger that we experience as an adult is merely a recycling of the anger that has its origins in the situations from our childhood and infancy. People do not get angry at the same things. This is because we all have our own unique menu of triggers for our anger, irritation and annoyance. These things are there because we have **ALREADY** experienced them.

The people we are angry with from childhood are usually those that have some power or authority over us. Our parents along with teachers, siblings and other relatives are therefore the ones that we hold most anger towards.

Anger and resentment are the main causes of breakdown in family relationships. It doesn't matter if we are eighteen or eighty, any anger that we have not released towards our parents will still be in evidence.

RELEASING ANGER

These negative feelings may drive a wedge between us and our parents that in many cases is never resolved.

When we release our anger towards our parents, we are able to have the type of relationship that we can only dream of. This does not mean presenting our parents with a list of things that we perceive that they did **WRONG**. It means taking responsibility for the creation of our feelings and deciding not to have them any more. Many people feel that letting their anger and resentment go would mean letting their parents off the hook. Their anger is the only way they feel they can punish their parents for their mistakes. Some people would rather die than absolve their parents for their actions.

Teenage years are a time when there is a great deal of anger in evidence. Parents and children get locked into a cycle of anger that can sometimes destroy the relationship permanently. It is important that parents deal with their anger away from the child at the same time making it all right for it to have the anger within certain boundaries.

RELEASING ANGER

When we do not resolve our anger with our parents we may end up recreating them in other areas of our lives. For instance a girl who has a controlling father may decide to get married to get away from his influence. It is likely that in some way her husband will mirror many aspects of her father and she may well end up experiencing the same anger she has for her father with her spouse. A man who has a dominant mother may find that he has a boss at work who treats him in exactly the same way that his mother did. He will then focus the anger he has for his mother on his boss.

ANGER AND OVERWEIGHT

Anger is an important factor in why we hold on to excess weight. Anger at trauma and abuse will often be a reason why the weight is put on in the first place. We can often notice that people put on weight after a difficult or life changing event in their lives.

Part of this process is about protection. The body may feel the need to protect us from our own anger. When there are toxins in the body, that due to overload are not processed by the liver, they need to be stored until a time when they can be processed. The poison is deactivated by being surrounded by either fat or fluid. Anger is just as toxic as any physical poisons and the body deals with it in similar ways. When we release the anger we allow the substance that is protecting us to be released as well since it is no longer needed.

There is another way in which anger and weight

are interlinked and this is with food. When we are angry or trying to avoid feeling our anger, we will often turn to food. Every time we eat without being hungry or if we cannot stop eating once we start, anger will probably be a factor. What we choose to eat is also very telling. When we are angry our body will usually crave sweet or savoury junk food, red meat, ice-cream, chocolate, refined or fatty products. When we eat these non nutritious foods we may have a few moments of satisfaction. However, a few minutes later we may be disgusted with ourselves and angry at our lack of will power. This in turn may make us eat some more in order to deaden these feelings. When we release the anger, we often find that our body craves good and healthy food and only as much as it needs. It is interesting to notice that we use words like **FED UP** to describe feelings of anger.

Our need to eat too much or the wrong food is often an indication that anger is about to emerge. If the anger is released at this point before the food is consumed, the weight can be released. It may be a good idea to put a note on the fridge or biscuit tin saying: **"WHO OR WHAT IS MAKING YOU ANGRY? RELEASE IT AND SEE IF YOU STILL WANT TO EAT."**

When we are overweight it will be necessary to look at the causes of our anger and to deal with them as well as the anger they have created. It will be a question of taking off the layers that have built up over the years.

DIS-EASE IN THE BODY

ON AN EMOTIONAL

LEVEL

CREATES DISEASE

IN THE BODY

ON A PHYSICAL LEVEL.

ALCOHOL, DRUGS AND CIGARETTES

Anger has a natural tendency to work its way to the surface. The body will always try to process and remove any substances that are toxic to it. When we do not want to have to deal with our anger, we have to find ways to prevent it from coming to the surface. As we have just seen food is one way that is often used to do this.

Alcohol, drugs and cigarettes are very effective ways that can keep anger at bay but at a great cost to the body. When we add this to the damage done by the anger itself, we can see how very destructive this pattern can be.

It must be pointed out that with alcohol, this can be counterproductive. While alcohol in moderation may well relax us and help with the stresses of our lives. As soon as we step over an invisible boundary and have the extra drink, the opposite effect might take place. Instead of keeping our anger at bay, it releases the control mechanisms that prevent us from using our anger in inappropriate ways. It is very easy to hurt someone or ourselves at this stage. The person who bears the brunt of our anger will usually have nothing to do with the creation of it.

The safe release of anger needs to become an integral part of dealing with addictions. Even though the actual addiction may be chemical, the trigger will usually be emotional.

PASSIVE AGGRESSION

Passive aggression is anger that does not materialise in an angry form. However, it may come out in ways that are every bit as destructive. It may be shown by what a person doesn't do rather than what they do. For instance a passive aggressive will not argue or row and yet their silence can incite the other person almost to the point of violence.

RELEASING ANGER

Many of the words and actions of the passive aggressive are aimed at making other people angry. For instance if a husband knows that when he leaves wet towels on the floor of the bathroom, his wife goes ballistic. He may continue to do this knowing that she is going to get angry. He may also feel that this action gives him a sense of power over her and he might even revel in his ability to make her furious. We tend to mirror each other in a relationship. The degree of anger that the one spouse displays is probably equal to the amount of anger the passive one is suppressing. When we encounter this particular cycle in a relationship, it is very destructive.

This form of aggression may also be in evidence in the teenage years. We are all familiar with the look of dumb insolence displayed by many adolescents. This look is enough to incite many parents to consider infanticide. Sulking can sometimes be a form of passive aggression and it always creates a negative reaction in those around.

ANGER IN RELATIONSHIPS

Unresolved anger and resentment is probably the number one cause of divorce and the break up of relationships. It becomes like a canker that eats away at the love, respect and attraction that are the foundations of the union. When these are destroyed it is very difficult to rebuild a structure strong enough to withstand the bombardment.

Relationships are our main opportunity for growth. Most issues that we have not dealt with from the past will surface in order to challenge us. All our unresolved baggage and anger with our parents is packed up and moved into the arena of our relationships. If we perceived that we did not get enough love, support, praise or respect from our parents then we will almost certainly find that pattern repeated with our spouse. The anger generated by our parents becomes compounded and aimed at our other half. Every time we fail to get our needs met in the relationship, we are angry with our partner, little realising that we do not have the right to expect and demand that they make us feel good about who we are.

We go into relationships thinking that we are going to get what we perceive we lack, such as love, security and nurturing. Part of our conditioning is the belief that if we find this special person, we will live happily ever after. There is often a great deal of anger when this particular illusion is shattered, as inevitably it is.

In a relationship we often desire to punish our partner with our anger. This may be done in very subtle ways. Withholding sex, leaving dirty clothes on the floor, not giving compliments, constantly criticising, refusing to do jobs when asked, the list is endless. The couple get locked into a cycle of anger and punishment until one side either chooses to get out or transform the relationship.

There is nothing worse than living in an atmosphere of anger all the time. In many relationships this anger is never expressed but it is always close to the surface and consequently it is picked up by anyone in the environment.

Signs of anger in a relationship are:
1) Not making eye contact.
2) Only ever talking about practicalities like the children or home.
3) Always appearing to be engrossed in television, the newspaper or a book when our partner is around.
4) No sex or only under duress.
5) Keeping busy all the time. Staying late at work or doing things around the home.
6) Making sure there are always other people around in social or leisure situations.
7) Going to bed at different times.
8) Nagging and criticising.
9) Not listening to what our partner has to say.
10) Mental, emotional or physical abuse.
11) Not finding anything good to say about our partner.

RELEASING ANGER

12) Feeling resentful for everything we do for our partner.
13) Sulking.
14) Flirting with other people, knowing that our partner can see.
15) Refusing to acknowledge that there is a problem when challenged.
16) Seething at or disagreeing with anything our partner says.

The good news is that it only takes one person in the relationship to turn it around and transform it. However, it is usually hard for one person to decide to do this without resenting the other for not participating.

The main part of this transformation involves releasing the anger. Our anger is our own and nothing to do with our partner. They only enabled it to come to the surface. They did **NOT** create it in the first place. While we blame others and make them responsible for our anger, we are not dealing with and releasing the actual issues involved.

ANGER AND SABOTAGE

We have the good fortune to create everything that happens to us and yet when we look around we see ourselves and others in dire situations and in a state of suffering and struggle. It is understandable that those who do not know about or understand our extraordinary creative power, find themselves in this position. However, those among us that are more enlightened and know that every thought and belief is creating our reality, are still finding ourselves in negative situations. Even when we have the knowledge to create the magic we do not do so. This may be because anger is a marvellous saboteur.

When we hold anger in our bodies it has nowhere to go but against us. On a physical level it will create illness. On a mental level it will fuel and empower our negative thoughts, creating negative situations that many people would simply dismiss as bad luck. There is no bad or good luck, there are only people creating what they believe in.

The victim inside us will be convinced that the Universe or God is **DOING** this to us, which will reinforce our sense of powerlessness.

Our anger creates situations where we make choices that are not in our best interest. This is often done completely unconsciously. Once we release our anger, when seemingly negative situations arise, instead of seeing it as proof of our being a victim, we can view it as a wonderful opportunity to learn, grow and expand.

Notice if you have a tendency to sabotage opportunities in your life. This may be a very good indication that there is some anger needing release.

ANGER AND GLOBAL ISSUES

For many people the only acceptable demonstration of anger is when it is against poverty, destruction of the environment or despotic governments. I have had people swear blind that they have no anger for themselves but it makes their blood boil when they see injustice, cruelty and abuse in the world. Anger is a subjective emotion. We do not have it if we have not had some direct experience of it. The person who rants and raves about injustice or cruelty will have had some injustice or cruelty in their childhood. The anger they display is actually about themselves. It is important to note that the source of our injustice may be very small in comparison with the global issues but it **FELT** every bit as strong at the time. For instance, if as a child, we got into trouble for something that a brother or sister had done, we might feel angry at the injustice of the situation.

When someone who has not experienced abuse

or injustice in their life views the global issues, they may be utterly appalled by what is going on in the world but they will not have the same degree of anger as someone who has the same issues.

It is a common practice to transfer our feelings from one source to another. I have often worked with clients who have been sexually abused and are in complete denial that they have any anger for the perpetrator. Yet when I ask how they feel if they read about or see a programme where a child has been sexually abused, they always reply that they are so angry that they could kill the person who did it to that child. This is a classic case of transference.

We often see people channelling their anger over the death of a loved one, whether through violence or illness, into fighting the cause for others. This form of anger is viewed by society as legitimate, even noble. We get the message from this that the only good expression of anger is on behalf of others.

It is essential that we learn to relate our anger to ourselves and face up to the situation that has caused it in the first place. We can only release our anger when we acknowledge and accept it. This way we can be set free from the tyranny of anger.

ANGER AND BEREAVEMENT

The process of bereavement goes through many phases and it is important to work through each of these in order to come out the other end and be able to participate fully in living again. Shock, numbness, guilt, grief and denial are all aspects of the loss.

Anger is also a very necessary part of bereavement. This is one area that some people fail to move through. Grief and guilt are feelings that are easy to accept, anger is not. We are angry with the person for dying, for leaving us and we may be angry with God or life for taking them from us. There is often a great deal of shame attached to feeling this and we don't dare to admit it to others and sometimes even to ourselves, let alone release it. This is particularly true when the person who dies went through a long or painful battle with illness. We feel selfish and guilty for harbouring anger towards them. When we do not deal with our anger we prolong the grieving process to years or even lifetimes. We may be prone to bouts of depression and life will be an uphill struggle from this point on.

Anger is natural when someone has died, it does not make us a bad person. The loved one has done something we didn't want them to do, they left us.

Once the anger around the death is released we are usually able to move through the rest of the grieving process unhindered.

PASSION

IS THE

POSITIVE

MANIFESTATION OF

ANGER.

FEAR OF ANGER

There is a great deal of fear around dealing with anger. I have found that many people believe that if they open up the can of worms marked "**ANGER**", they are going to turn into an axe murderer and destroy everything in the vicinity. They know or suspect the destructive power that this emotion has and they are afraid of it.

Society tells us that the only way to deal with anger is to control it, to shut it away and have nothing to do with it. We are led to believe that if we don't do this, we will become out of control and probably end up in a prison or a mental home. The reality is, in fact, quite the opposite. If we repress our anger we are turning that destructive force against ourselves and we are in danger of a person triggering our anger to such an extent that we **DO** lose control.

If we are aware of the anger inside us, we are also aware that in a moment of temper or anger we could easily kill someone and this frightens us. We may be condemning a murderer for their actions knowing that, there but for the grace of God, go we. This knowledge will usually make us bottle up our anger still further.

If we safely and gently release our anger, this situation would not and could not occur. Very often we believe we are protecting those around us by withholding our anger when in reality we are endangering them.

LEVELS AND LAYERS OF ANGER

Our anger builds up over the years and in releasing it we need to be aware that this is an ongoing process. When we release the anger that has come to the surface, we will notice a difference for a while. Then the next layer will emerge. We can steadily do our anger work as each level or layer appears.

RELEASING ANGER

Much of our anger will stem from certain incidents, traumas, and dialogue that have occurred in childhood. From this point on every time someone or something mirrors those initial incidents, we will feel anger. Each repetition of this pattern will create a layer of anger that will be added to the others. We may choose to deal with our anger each time it is triggered and release it safely. However this does nothing to remove the original source of the anger and this will continue to emerge each time that particular button is pressed.

We can deal with our anger by removing all the buttons or triggers that we have from childhood. This is achieved by allowing the anger to be released at source. This in effect is shutting off the stop cock instead of constantly dealing with the result of the flood. When we resolve the initial anger, not only do we remove the triggers for our anger but all the subsequent anger in between can be released.

DEALING WITH ANGER

Releasing anger is part of a purification process. The purpose of letting anger go is in order not to have any anger in our lives and to allow love, joy, fun and happiness to become our primary emotions.

When a child shouts at its mother "I hate you", in that moment it means it. However, as soon as this feeling is expressed, it is gone and the child is able to love its mother freely. If that feeling is not allowed to be expressed, then that hate is then stored in the body and does untold damage. When we release anger safely we may express thoughts or feeling that seem to be wrong or bad. We are doing this in order that they need not exist any longer.

If the adult aspect of ourselves judges our anger and finds it to be bad or shameful, then we will not allow ourselves to get rid of it. Our anger is there as a result of our damage and the only way to heal that damage is to express our **TRUTH**. If our truth was that at that moment that we hated our mother or father, it is imperative that we are honest about it if only to ourselves and release the feeling. We are then free to genuinely love that person instead of pretending to.

When we release our anger safely, we do not hurt the person involved. We are in fact hurting them far more by not holding on to the anger.

Many people believe that it would be wrong to voice or acknowledge the feelings of anger as this would send a negative message to the Universe. The fact is that these thoughts already exist and are creating negative situations in our lives that perpetuate the negativity. When we **EXPRESS** the feeling with either the written or spoken word, then the anger does not exist any more.

ANGER AND FORGIVENESS

Forgiveness will heal anything. It heals relationships, illnesses, grudges and grievances. However, we cannot forgive on top of anger. The path to forgiveness is to release the anger first. We can do forgiveness affirmations until the cows come home but the underlying feeling will not have changed. It is like putting a plaster over a festering sore and expecting it to heal. We must first of all clean out and purify the canker and then use the forgiveness to be instrumental in the healing process.

When we put out the intention of healing a relationship or situation, we will often find that any anger that is getting in the way will be brought to our attention in order that it may be healed.

ANGER AND HURT

We often use anger to protect ourselves from feeling our emotional pain. We may perceive our hurt to be vulnerable and that can seem to be a weak response. Anger will appear to be a much more powerful energy and therefore come from a position of strength.

This can be a predominantly male energy pattern and it can create a great deal of misunderstanding. We lose sight of the fact that many people showing anger are really upset and hurt by the situation. When we are faced with a person's anger, we may respond by being angry and defensive and so conflict may result.

Many women have a similar problem with expressing anger. They will often cry when they are angry and this may seem to be weak. However, when we show our pain we are more likely to get a positive response from others. They may want to comfort us or to remove the thing that is causing us pain.

We need to be prepared for the fact that when we begin to release our anger, we may also get in touch with the hurt that is lying beneath it. This is actually a very positive thing but for people who spend their life trying to avoid feeling hurt, this may not seem to be the case.

ANGER AND POWERLESSNESS

One of the most prominent feelings we have around anger is powerlessness. Anger is created out of **OTHER** people doing or not doing something. We therefore have no power or control over their actions

Virtually all anger that we have has its source in childhood. When we are a baby or small child, we seem to be genuinely powerless. We are dependent on adults for our very survival. We do not have the means to communicate our needs in a cohesive form and we are severely limited in our ability to make the things we want happen.

When we experience anger as an adult, we feel it as we did when we **FIRST** felt it. Consequently, the feelings of powerlessness are attached to our anger. This sense of powerlessness can totally paralyse us. We feel as if we can do nothing to change the situation we find ourselves in. We may also feel the vulnerability that the child had at the time.

The reality is that as an adult we have total power over our own lives. We can recognise that we do not have the right to demand that another person does what we want them to. We may rationalise the situation with our thinking rather than our feeling part. We also have the problem solving skills which can find the perfect solution to any issue.

When we believe ourselves to be powerless, this is exactly what **WE** create in our world. It is important to remember that this is an illusion and we can take our power back just by **CHOOSING** to see the situation differently.

ANGER
AND PASSION

Anger is a very powerful energy. How this energy manifests is totally dependent on the type of charge that we put into it. If we put a negative charge on it then it will become destructive either to ourselves or others. However, simply by changing the polarity of the charge and making it positive, we turn it into passion.

Passion is a wonderful feeling and it can be channelled into many different areas of life. If we put it into our relationships, we raise them to a higher level. Many couples find that when they have a row, this heightens their senses to such a degree that the making up is very passionate. They may even create a row in order to reach the passion. This route is totally unnecessary and the anger can erode the relationship.

When we have passion for our lifework or hobbies, we find that we are more productive. This powerful energy can move mountains. We can also find that we are not drained or exhausted from our exertions. Instead we almost feel as if we have more energy.

When we suppress anger we also suppress our passion. It is rare to see a depressed person become passionate about anything. It is our choice as to which charge we decide to put on our energy and how it manifests in our lives.

THE SPECTRUM OF ANGER

Anger covers a large spectrum of feeling from mild irritation to fury. Obviously the destructive nature of the feeling will depend where on the scale we are.

We will look at the various grades of anger that we may experience. At the lower end of the scale we have annoyance, irritation, frustration, pissed off and heated. At the upper end of the scale, we may feel livid, incandescent with rage, furious and hate.

RELEASING ANGER

Some of these manifestations are ongoing while others are more explosive. The more volcanic of these are without doubt more dangerous but they are usually short lived. We may live with our anger simmering away for many years.

When we are in touch with the higher end of the anger scale particularly with hatred, rage and fury, we can become totally out of control. The feeling is so strong that it takes us over and we are unable to think or act rationally. We are in effect blinded by our rage and may do things that we regret later.

Many people try to downgrade their anger to a level that seems more acceptable and they can cope with. For instance, a woman who is boiling with rage may describe herself as being a little bit annoyed. This is a form of denial and can result in our not dealing with the whole issue.

ANGER AND ACCEPTANCE

The ultimate goal with anger is not to have any. This is achieved by releasing all the old stored up anger inside. We then remove all the buttons and triggers from our unconscious minds, so that we do not react angrily when we are faced with situations that mirror the ones that created our initial anger.

The next stage of this process is to begin to live consciously. This means that in every moment we choose how we think, feel and believe. Acceptance is the key part of this. When we accept ourselves, other people and situations just as they are, we are liberated to experience joy and happiness no matter what is going on.

As adults we can recognise that we have only the right to control ourselves and our own lives. Anger is created out of the actions or inaction of others. As soon as we are able to **ACCEPT** the behaviour of others, we do not need to experience any anger in our lives.

The next step after acceptance is the knowledge that everything that happens to us is **ALWAYS** for our highest good. It may be there to show us some damage from the past that needs to be released or healed. It could also be the catalyst that moves us forward or puts us in the place that we are meant to be, in order to progress to the next level of our development.

Acceptance is something that is only achieved with practice and commitment. It does not happen if we don't put effort into it.

ACCEPTANCE
IS THE
KEY
TO
HAPPINESS.

PART 2

DEALING WITH
AND
RELEASING
ANGER.

ANGER AND
THE LAWS OF RELEASE

Anger can be very powerful. It is rather like dynamite. In the wrong hands it may be deadly but at the same time it can be a very useful commodity. Anger expressed inappropriately can be extremely destructive. Anger that is not expressed is very self-destructive. At the same time anger can also be the motivational force behind campaigns to make this world a better place to live in. Anger can be a form of passion that inspires others to make a difference in their lives and therefore the world.

SAFETY IS THE MAIN EMPHASIS IN RELEASING ANGER.

The three main rules of anger release are:
1)   **DO NOT HURT OTHERS** – This means that we do not hurt others physically, mentally or emotionally with our anger. This includes pets and animals.

RELEASING ANGER

2) **DO NOT HURT YOURSELF** – This includes the non release of anger, which will ultimately hurt oneself. Equally self-mutilation, reckless behaviour or putting your fist through a wall or window is not an advisable way of dealing with anger.

3) **DO NOT DESTROY ANYTHING** – Smashing plates or trashing property may feel good in the moment but there are consequences to these actions. You will always end up paying for it either financially or with a police record.

It is **RARELY** productive to express our anger to the person with whom we are angry. Firstly, that person is not the one that we are actually angry with and our anger will be out of proportion to the situation. Secondly, our anger will probably activate the other person's anger and defensiveness and this will either be dumped straight back onto us or they will take it out on someone else. This perpetuates the anger on the planet. It simply recycles the emotion instead of getting rid of it. When someone is confrontational and angry we do not take in **WHAT** they are saying merely **HOW** they are saying it.

RELEASING ANGER

When we are in a situation where we become angry and are intent on resolving it with the other person, it is advisable to follow certain steps.

1) Take responsibility for your own anger, i.e. don't say - He/she **MADE** me angry.

2) Remove yourself from the situation until you have understood the real dynamic.

3) Ask yourself what this person or situation was there to show you. Who are they representing? i.e. a parent or spouse. What was it about the situation that made you angry?

4) Release this anger safely. You may find you need to release it about the person it really concerns.

5) When you are calm and clear about the occurrence then you can discuss it with the person involved. Make sure your intention is to resolve the problem and not to blame or punish the person.

6) You may find that simply by releasing the anger the situation has resolved itself.

7) It is only productive to confront the person, if doing so will empower them.

REMOVING ANGER FROM OUR LIVES

It is perfectly possible to completely remove anger from our lives. This does not mean that we simply push it down so that we do not feel it or experience it. We want to completely eliminate anger from the mind, body and soul.

There are so many taboos around anger and we are often afraid of bringing it up and letting it out. Anger is a very ugly emotion and consequently we do not want to voluntarily experience it or show it to other people. However the ugliness of anger will be in evidence somewhere in our lives if we do not release and remove it. A few minutes of ugliness is a small price to pay for a lifetime of peace, harmony and beauty.

Anger is a feeling and in order for it to be released we need to <u>feel</u> it. Many of us try to deal with and release anger without actually feeling it. We may even convince ourselves that we have done so. The most common way we believe that we have dealt with our anger is through the mind. We are very good at thinking and talking about our anger. We may believe that if we release the **THOUGHTS ABOUT** anger, then the anger is also gone and dealt with.

Another way in which we think we would like to get rid of our anger is on a spiritual level. We may believe that if we ask our guides or helpers to remove the anger then this is done. We may also think that it can be removed in meditations or visualisations. The fact is that when we go into a meditative or **DIVINE** state, we elevate ourselves above our baser feelings and thoughts. This may give an illusion that we have let them go. This method could only work if we manage to remain in the **DIVINE** mode at all times and this is a very tall order.

Our ability to remove anger from our lives is going to depend on certain things.

1)   We remove any denial about our anger.

RELEASING ANGER

2) A willingness to allow ourselves to experience our anger in order to let it go.

3) Sending out the intention to our emotional body to let our anger surface in gentle easy ways.

4) We welcome any unreleased anger being brought to our attention.

5) We thank the person or situation that has brought it to our attention.

6) As soon as we have connected with our anger we can let it go immediately.

7) When the anger is released, we can return to feeling normal.

8) We need to learn the lesson that the anger is there to convey. If this is not done we may only have to go through the same process all over again.

9) We can make sure there are no residue negative feelings for the person that triggered the anger.

ANGER AWARENESS

Anger is almost always a REaction. We act as we have done before in similar circumstances. When we react, we are doing so unconsciously, the pattern will play out without us consciously deciding what to think or feel. It is important that we become aware of our patterns and triggers with anger. When this is done we can notice when these particular triggers are about to spring. We can then pre-empt our anger and decide if this is how we would like to create this moment. Once we are aware of our triggers we can also work on removing them at source.

We can also be aware of the signs that anger is about to surface. (see HOW TO RECOGNISE ANGER.) If we notice that we have become very sluggish and tired or we keep trying to escape from the realities of our lives or we keep cutting or burning ourselves, this may be an indication that anger is an issue that is about to reach our consciousness. When we do not spot the signs at this early stage, we may actually allow a full blown situation to arise that is guaranteed to bring up our anger.

Most of the anger that emerges is well removed from the original source and consequently we end up focusing it on the person or situation that brought it to our attention, rather than what it is really about. It is a bit like killing the messenger that brings the bad news. At the end of the day the news is still the same and has not actually been dealt with.

When anger is a feature in our lives we can be aware of it by following these points:

1) Note the signs that show that anger is about to emerge.
2) Have a willingness to deal with it before it erupts in an inappropriate manner.
3) At what point did these symptoms begin to emerge?
4) What was going on before or around this time?
5) Who was involved?
6) What was said or done or not done that tapped into the anger?
7) If the anger appeared suddenly, what happened at the time?
8) Is this a pattern that you are aware of?

RELEASING ANGER

9) What did you think or feel about yourself as a result of the incident?

10) Did you take out your anger on the person who brought it up?

11) Did you take out your anger on someone other than the one who brought it up?

12) Did you try to push down and suppress the anger when it emerged?

13) What was the exact trigger for the anger, put it in a cohesive form? For instance, "My boss made me angry because he blamed me for his own incompetence." or "I am angry with my husband because he treats me like a slave and gives me no praise for what I do."

14) Notice how this fits into your patterning. There may be issues of unworthiness or low self-esteem. When we have these patterns we will tend to attract people into our lives who will reinforce them.

15) Be aware that this is something that is unhealed in your life and it needs to be dealt with in order for you to cease creating it.

16) Release the anger that has been brought up in a <u>safe</u> way.

METHODS OF RELEASE

There are many ways that we can release our anger safely at the point where it comes to the surface. The reality is that we do not need to feel or experience our anger for more than a few moments before releasing it. However many people will choose to sit with it for years or even a lifetime. This is completely unnecessary and somewhat masochistic. Anger is an unattractive emotion and we sometimes hold onto it rather than show this ugliness to the world. It is really important to note that we do not need to show it to anyone else. The willingness to let our anger go is all that is needed.

It is the **EXPRESSION** of anger that is going to remove it from our bodies and our lives. This expression can take place in many different ways, some more tangible than others. I will show some of the means by which we can remove anger and its destructive side effects.

BREATHING

The most effective things in life are often the simplest. With anger release our breath is key. It is not only the thing that connects us with the feeling it is also the means by which we can let it go.

The fact is that very few of us know how to breathe properly. We only use a small percentage of our lung capacity. We often only use the upper part of our lungs. We can check to see how we breathe by watching what part of the body moves when we take a deep breath. If our upper chest moves and our shoulders go up, then we are shallow breathers. If our stomach inflates when we breathe and our upper chest does not then we are using the full capacity of our lungs.

There are many different reasons why we do not breathe properly. With some people it is habit, they may not have learned how to breathe. The most common reason for not breathing deeply is totally unconscious. Our feeling centre is the solar plexus. In order to feel our feelings we need to breathe into this part. If we are uncomfortable with our feelings, we will make sure that do not allow our breath to access them.

Another way in which we do not breathe properly is that we put more stress on breathing in than we do breathing out. This means that our lungs are often filled with stale unusable air that does not get expired. The out breath is more important than the in breath because nature abhors a vacuum. If we create a space then this will **AUTOMATICALLY** be filled with fresh oxygenated air.

In using the breath to release our anger, it is essential that we access the feeling with our breathing. This may involve deepening the breath to connect with the solar plexus. When the anger has been touched, it is equally important to release it on the breath. This means exhaling as strongly and powerfully as possible and to keep on doing this until feelings of peace and calm replace those of anger.

RELEASING ANGER

It is almost as if the breath acts as a vehicle that attaches to the anger and is the means by which it can leave the body.

This is a very simple and powerful technique that if employed as soon as we become aware of the anger can insure that it does not have a detrimental effect in our lives.

To recap:
1) When anger surfaces, deepen the breath.
2) Access the anger by taking the breath to the place where it is in the body.
3) Expel the air with the anger attached forcefully from the body.
4) Repeat this until there is no more anger to clear out from the solar plexus.
5) The breath will come out smoothly and gently.

PHYSICAL EXPRESSION

Physical expression of anger can be a very effective means of release but it is essential that this is done safely and is not allowed to get out of control.

Anger is an emotion. (Energy in motion.) It is therefore very powerful when we put movement into our expression of anger. Anger is also in the physical body so it makes sense to release it on this level.

However, the physical expression of anger is very destructive and it is essential to follow the rules of anger release if we use this method.

1) **Do not hurt others.**
2) **Do not hurt yourself.**
3) **Do not destroy property.**

Our natural reaction in expressing our anger physically it to use our arms or legs. We want to hit or kick out. We do not want to hurt others by putting a fist in their face. When hitting out we do not want to hurt ourselves by jarring our joints or bashing our hands or knuckles. We also do not want to break or damage anything. We want to use something soft to cushion the effect of our anger and we also want to use some instrument instead of our hands or legs.

The easiest and most effective way of releasing our anger physically is to put some cushions or pillows on a bed and to use a baseball bat or some other pole or old tennis racket. Make sure there is nothing that might be hit like light fixtures. Some people use a length of hose on a pile of telephone directories. We can also use a punch bag or ball but make sure that gloves are used or we may end up hurting our hands.

Once again we need to use the breath to help access the feelings of anger and release them. This technique is more effective if used in conjunction with verbal expression.

Steps for releasing anger physically.
1)	Decide who or what you are most angry about.
2)	Find a safe space where you will not be

      disturbed and you will not disturb anyone else. Make sure the person you are angry with is not around. Keep animals and children away for this.

3) Set up the arena for your expression. Ensure that there is nothing that will be damaged.

4) Before you start to express your anger, make sure you are in your body and not your mind. Breathe into your solar plexus. You may even need to jump up and down or do something physical in order to be in the body.

5) Focus on the person or reason for your anger and then begin to hit out.

6) Keep going until you feel your anger is spent.

7) When you access your anger, you may also find there is some pain and sadness attached. Allow these feelings to come up as well.

Some people use sport as a means of releasing and dealing with anger. Rugby, tennis squash, football and many other contact sports will often be effective in taking the top off our anger.

VERBAL EXPRESSION

This is another effective means of release. It can be used along side other techniques or on its own. When we use the voice we access the feelings and have a built in means of expression. The verbal expression needs to be loud and to sound angry. This is done most effectively along with the physical release. When we are hitting out, we put words with the movements. In a way this is similar to using the breath for release. When we are shouting, we take a deep breath and the sound is released on the breath.

We are often very self-conscious about expressing our anger verbally, this may act as a deterrent to this form of release. The car is one place that might seem a safe place to do this. The physical structure of the car acts as a barrier between us and the world, we feel as if we are anonymous and that other people cannot hear us.

RELEASING ANGER

This method can be very effective for children, it can be made to feel like a game at the same time as letting go any pent up anger or frustration.

There is another technique for releasing anger verbally and physically. We focus our anger energy into our fists, then we open our arms and hands at the same time as emitting a shout. The energy is then released out through the palms of the hand as well as through the mouth. This can be repeated until we can no longer find any anger to put into our fists.

WRITTEN EXPRESSION

This method of release can be very effective and is often used by those who do not like the more confrontational means of dealing with anger.

The main way of doing this is anger burn letters. Here we express our feelings on paper to the person that we are angry with. We do not give them the letter, instead we burn it and release the feelings and thoughts that are contained in it. One of the reasons that this method is so effective is that when we are angry we tend to go over and over in our mind about the situation or person involved. Our thoughts then constantly fuel the anger and so the cycle goes on. However, when we commit our thoughts to paper our mind is able to let go of them. It is like when we are going out shopping and we have the list of what we need in our head. We keep going over it and repeating it in our mind, making sure that we don't forget any of our needs. As soon as we write the list down, the brain is able to release it. Similarly when we list our feelings and thoughts we do not need to have them anymore.

When we become aware of our anger and the person it has been triggered by, we can use anger letters to release this feeling.

Tips for anger burn letters.
1)   Who is the person that the anger is aimed at?
2)   What are the circumstances that have brought up your anger?

3) As soon as you are aware of these things, take some time to do your release.

4) Remove yourself from other people and get some paper to write on.

5) Remember that your anger is coming from the child aspect of yourself, so the thoughts and feelings may seem very childish and petty. Do not try and put an adult analysis onto your anger as this will remove you from the actual feelings.

6) When a child is angry it often just says **I HATE YOU** or calls you names. Use this technique. Often, the most effective burn letters will repeat the same statement again and again until this thought is expressed to such an extent that it is no longer true.

7) If you are having problems accessing the child's feelings use your left or non dominant hand to write. Not only will the writing appear to be childish but it will feel it too.

8) You may also find it effective to scribble all

over the letter as a means of expressing the anger in a childish mode.

9) It is helpful to end the letter with a resolution like:

   I choose to let my anger go in order that I may love you unconditionally. or, **I release my anger with love.**

10) Burn the letter outside. A metal bucket is probably the safest receptacle. You may feel the feelings go as you watch the paper burn. If the letter does not burn easily, it may be an indication that you are not willing to completely let your feelings go. You may need to repeat the process.

NEVER SHOW THE LETTER TO THE PERSON INVOLVED.

DON'T hold onto the letter, burn it as soon as possible, this shows that you are ready to move on.

DEALING WITH ANGER IN CHILDREN

Since most of our anger is created in childhood, we can avoid a great many problems later in life by teaching our children about anger and how to release it safely. We usually end up recreating the same taboos around anger that we experienced as children. It is essential that we begin to stop the destructive cycle of anger and suppression that is causing most of the problems that are in the world as a whole.

If children are taught that anger is not wrong or bad but the inappropriate expression of it is, then we can show them ways to release and deal with their anger that is not going to create problems for them in later life.

When a child is angry, instead of reacting to them with anger or to punish them, try the following tips:

1) Ask or find out **WHY** they are angry without making them wrong for their anger.

2) They will probably be angry with you, so do not become defensive or guilty.

3) Validate their right to have their anger in that situation, without necessarily changing it.

4) Admit and accept if you have in some way disempowered them and say you are sorry.

5) Empathise with their anger. Let them know that you would probably have felt angry in the same situation. Explain to the child the situation and help them to understand why it is the way it is. For instance, if a child is punished for running out into the road, it will be angry. If it is explained to the child that the parent was reacting to their fear of it being run over, then the whole perception of the situation can change.

6) Show the child how to release and express their anger in a safe way. (See methods of release.) Give the child permission to be angry with you and make the method of release seem like a game.

7) Make sure that the child is aware of how it is inappropriate to express anger, without making the anger bad or wrong.

RELEASING THE SOURCE OF ANGER

All the techniques we have shown are designed to release anger as and when it surfaces. However, none of these actually deals with the underlying cause of the anger. It is like trying to deal with a leak simply by catching and throwing out the water that escapes. It is only when we find and mend the source of the leak that we no longer need to constantly clear up after the effects.

The source of most anger is in childhood, usually in the first seven years. This is when we are working predominantly with our feelings. We will find that the sources of most of our anger are from tiny incidents that any adult would not even notice. However, these patterns become bigger each time they are repeated. When we are adults they may be very big indeed.

We have every age of child that we have ever been within our unconscious mind. Every time we were not able to express our anger at the point where it was created, we will have a button that may be pushed each time we experience a similar situation. In order to remove the button or trigger we need to allow the child that was unable to release the anger at the time to do so. We therefore simply need to find out the source of the anger and let the little one inside express itself in a safe way. Once this is done, the anger trigger can be removed.

We work with the unconscious mind to find out the original situation that caused the anger. The unconscious mind can connect with us through the feeling side of ourselves. This simply means accessing the information away from the thinking mind. Most of the incidents occurred before we have any conscious memory. Simply by asking the unconscious mind questions that have a yes or no answer, we can find out what has created the anger. We then allow the child to express the feeling at source. There are no reprisals or punishment from doing this and no one can be hurt from our anger.

RELEASING ANGER

The process for releasing anger at source.

1) When anger has been brought to your attention, look at what the trigger for it has been.

2) Put this into a cohesive statement. For instance, "When someone criticises or judges me, I feel angry."

3) It is the source of this particular pattern that you will be looking for.

4) You are working with your unconscious mind to find the source of this. It will connect with you through feelings and not thoughts. This is the feeling when you know you know something, without knowing how or why.

5) Ask your unconscious mind to take you back in time to the age you were when this pattern and the anger was first created.

6) Ask you unconscious mind what age you were at the time.

7) Where were you, at home or somewhere else?

8) Was it day or night?

RELEASING ANGER

9) Were you in a living or bedroom area?
10) Who was there, mother, father or siblings?
11) What are you doing?
12) What has been done or not done to make you angry?
13) Who are you angry with?
14) Allow yourself to express the anger in your mind to the person involved.
15) Breathe the anger out and away from the body until you no longer feel it.
16) Do not worry about what you do or say in expressing your anger, you will not hurt the person in reality.
17) Ask your unconscious mind to remove this pattern from the mind and memory bank.
18) Instate acceptance or forgiveness into the situation in order to heal the original situation.
19) Change the situation in your mind so that the child feels good.
20) Bring this sense of peace and calm forward in time into this present moment.

21) In your mind thank the person that brought
your unhealed anger to your attention. Allow
the feelings you have toward this person to
dissipate.

You may want to get someone to help you with this
process or put it on tape. The more experienced you
become with working with the unconscious mind the
easier it will become. You can use this technique
every time your anger is triggered and brought to the
surface.

THE EFFECTS OF RELEASING ANGER

Releasing anger safely will transform our lives
on so many levels. Our relationships with friends,
family and partners will improve immeasurably. We
will even like and love ourselves more. Our health will
get better. We may even find that our creativity
increases or begins to emerge. Our prospects can
also improve.

RELEASING ANGER

The object of anger release is to eventually have no more anger to express. We begin to notice that situations that used to ignite our anger before, no longer do so. When there is nothing to trigger a reaction, we can begin to decide how we want to respond to each situation as and when it arises.

Our evolved and adult selves know that we have no right to demand that another person behave or react in a certain way. We therefore have no need for anger, only an acceptance that everything that appens to us is perfect just as it is. We cannot control people or situations therefore it is pointless to be angry when we fail to do so.

I wish you all a life free from the tyranny of anger!

HAVE A NEW RELEASE OF LIFE.